Scott, Foresman Reading

# Kick Up Your Heels

**Program Authors**

Ira E. Aaron
Dauris Jackson
Carole Riggs
Richard G. Smith
Robert J. Tierney

**Book Authors**

Robert E. Jennings
Dorothy E. Prince

**Instructional Consultants**

John Manning
Dolores Perez

Scott, Foresman and Company
Editorial Offices: Glenview, Illinois

Regional Offices: Palo Alto, California
Tucker, Georgia • Glenview, Illinois
Oakland, New Jersey • Dallas, Texas

## ACKNOWLEDGMENTS

"Drinking Fountain" from RHYMES ABOUT THE CITY by Marchette Chute. Copyright 1946 (Macmillan), renewal 1974 by Marchette Chute. Reprinted by permission of the author.

"Play" from COUNTRY PIE by Frank Asch. Copyright © 1979 by Frank Asch. By permission of Greenwillow Books (A Division of William Morrow & Company).

"The Ducks" by Alice Wilkins from THE GOLDEN FLUTE: An Anthology of Poetry for Young Children, selected by Alice Hubbard and Adeline Babbitt. Copyright 1932, 1960 by Harper & Row, Publishers, Inc. A John Day Book. By permission of Thomas Y. Crowell, Publishers.

"Clouds" and "The Mouse and the Winds" from MOUSE TALES by Arnold Lobel. Copyright © 1972 by Arnold Lobel. By permission of Harper & Row, Publishers, Inc. and World's Work Limited, The Windmill Press.

"Jump or Jiggle" by Evelyn Beyer from ANOTHER HERE AND NOW STORY BOOK edited by Lucy Sprague Mitchell. Copyright, 1937, by E. P. Dutton & Co., Inc. Copyright renewal © 1965 by Lucy Sprague Mitchell. Reprinted by permission of the publisher, E. P. Dutton.

"One of Each, Please," from OPEN THE DOOR by Marion Edey. Copyright 1949 by Marion Edey and Dorothy Grider. Reprinted by permission of Charles Scribner's Sons.

"Mr. Gumpy's Motor Car" consists of the adapted text and selected illustrations from MR. GUMPY'S MOTOR CAR written and illustrated by John Burningham. Copyright © 1973 by John Burningham. By permission of Thomas Y. Crowell, Publishers and Jonathan Cape Limited.

"Very Lovely" from FAIRY GREEN by Rose Fyleman. Copyright 1923 by George H. Doran. Reprinted by permission of Doubleday & Company, Inc. and the Society of Authors as the literary representative of the Estate of Rose Fyleman.

Glossary entries taken or adapted from MY FIRST PICTURE DICTIONARY. Copyright © 1975, 1970 Scott, Foresman and Company. All Rights Reserved. Also from MY SECOND PICTURE DICTIONARY. Copyright © 1975, 1971 Scott, Foresman and Company. All Rights Reserved.

(acknowledgments continued on page 272)

ISBN 0–673–21408–7

2345678910-RMI-908988878685

# CONTENTS

## SECTION TWO

# SECTION ONE

# The Bird and the Pitcher

a fable by Aesop
adapted by William H. Hooks

One time there was a mother bird.
She had three little birds.
She looked after her little ones.
She found good things to eat.
She found good water to drink.
She would sing to her little birds.
Singing was good for the little ones.
But eating was much better.
They wanted to eat and drink all
the time.

8

One day the mother bird could not find
any water.
She looked and looked.
She looked all day.
She went home to her little birds.

"Can we have some water?" they asked.

"I can't find any," said the mother.

"No water?" the little birds asked.
"We have not had a drink all day!"

The next day the mother bird went off as soon as it was light.

"I must find water for my little ones," she said.
"And I need water too."

This time she went far away.
She asked the people she saw for water.
No one had any water to give her.

"What can I do?" she asked.

10

At last the mother bird came home.
The little ones were jumping up and down.

"What is going on?" asked the mother.

"We know where there is water!" they
called.

"Where?" asked the mother bird.

"Over there," said the little ones.
The mother bird looked behind her.
There was a big pitcher.
Would there be good, cold water in it?

"How did this pitcher get here?" the mother bird asked her little ones.

"We saw a boy leave it," they said.

The mother ran over to the pitcher.

"There is some water in it," she said.

"But we can't get the water out," said one little bird.
"The water is too far down in the pitcher."

12

The mother bird looked all about.
She saw some small stones.

"Give me those stones," she said.

The little birds ran to get the stones.

"What are the stones for?" they asked.

"Look," said the mother bird.
She picked up a stone and put it in
the pitcher.
The water came up a little in the
pitcher.
So she put in more and more stones.

"Look!" said the little birds.
"The water is going to come out!"

The mother bird put in one more stone.

"Come and drink now," she called.

The three little birds and their mother
had a good drink.

One little bird asked, "Mother, how did
you do it?"

"Put your head to work, and you will
find a way," said the happy mother bird.

**Comprehension Check**
1. How did the mother bird look after
   her little ones?
2. How would you get the water if there
   were no stones?

# The Drinking Fountain

by Marchette Chute

When I climb up
To get a drink,
It doesn't work
The way you'd think.

I turn it up,
The water goes
And hits me right
Upon the nose.

I turn it down
To make it small
And don't get any
Drink at all.

# What I Have to Give

a Norwegian folk tale
adapted by Peter Martin Wortmann

Kim and Pat lived side by side.
They ran and played and laughed side
by side too.

One day Pat said to Kim, "I can't play
with you today.
I am going to buy some things.
I want to buy something new for you."

16

Kim did not want Pat to go.

"This is a good day to play," said Kim.
"I don't need something new."

But Pat went off.

"Now, what would Kim like to have?"
asked Pat as he walked.
"He would like a big, pretty orange."

Pat found the oranges.
He looked at all the oranges.
He took one that looked good.

"This is a big, pretty orange!
I'll buy it for Kim," he said.

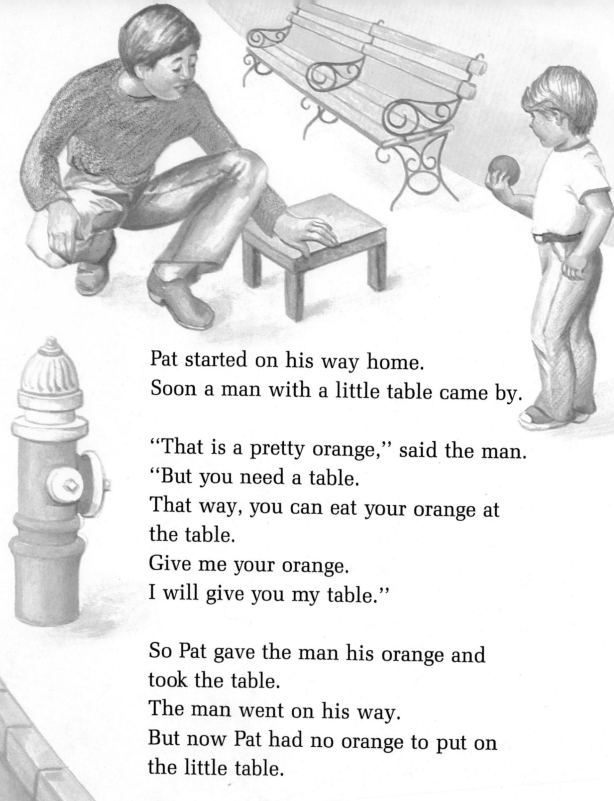

Pat started on his way home.
Soon a man with a little table came by.

"That is a pretty orange," said the man.
"But you need a table.
That way, you can eat your orange at
the table.
Give me your orange.
I will give you my table."

So Pat gave the man his orange and
took the table.
The man went on his way.
But now Pat had no orange to put on
the little table.

18

"I'll give Kim this table," said Pat.
"He will be happy to have it."

So Pat started home with the table.
Soon a girl with a book came by.

"If you give me that table," she said,
"I will give you this book.
That way, you will have a good book
to put on your table."

Pat took the girl's book and gave her
the table.
The girl went on her way.
But now Pat had no table for the book.

Pat started home one more time.
Soon he came to an old man.

"I would like to have a book like
that one," said the man.

"But what can you give me?" asked Pat.

"I will give you the best thing of all,"
said the man.
"I will give you this pretty day."

So Pat gave the man his book.
The man went on his way.

20

At last Pat came to Kim's house.
There was not one thing in his hands.
Pat wished he had his orange.

"Did you get me something?" asked Kim.

Pat told Kim about the orange.
He told Kim about the people he saw.

"Now all I have to give you is this
pretty day," said Pat.

"But that is the best thing of all!"
said Kim.

So Kim and Pat ran and laughed.
They played and played all that pretty
day.

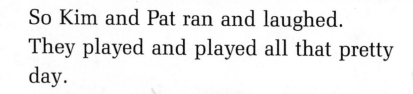

**Comprehension Check**

1. What things did Pat get for Kim?
2. How do you know that Kim was happy with the pretty day?

# PLAY

by Frank Asch

"Come play with me," said the sun.
"Come play with me," said the earth.
"Come play with me," said the sky.
"What shall we play?" said I.
"Let's fly a kite," said the sun.
"Stand on me," said the earth.
"I'll bring the wind," said the sky.
"I'll hold the string," said I.

# Look Out for Mr. Quills

by William H. Hooks

There is no other animal like Mr. Quills.
He has brown and white fur.
He looks like he is full of toothpicks.
What is he?
Give up?
He is a porcupine!

Mr. Quills is a good name for a
porcupine.
His fur is full of long, sharp quills.
Don't play with Mr. Quills.
You could get hurt.

24

Mr. Quills lives where it is cold.
He lives where there are many trees.
He likes to sit for a long time in
the trees.
Mr. Quills can sit in one tree for
many days.
He eats the tree's bark.
He will hurt the tree if he eats too
much of the bark.

Mr. Quills has small feet.
He can't run far.
He can't run away if there is a fight.
So what can Mr. Quills do in a fight?
His many long, sharp quills are a
big help.
Not many animals will fight with a
porcupine.
Other animals do not want to get next
to the quills.

Some animals do not know about those
long, sharp quills.
They will run after porcupines.
This can start a fight.

If an animal jumps on a porcupine,
the animal will stop right away.
The animal's feet will hurt.
They will be full of sharp quills.

This dog jumped on a porcupine.
The quills hurt the dog's feet.
The dog ran to a girl right away.
She saw the dog's feet.
They were full of quills.
The girl picked out the quills.
Now the dog's feet do not hurt.
This dog will not fight any other
porcupines for a long time.

28

## How to Make a Porcupine

Would you like to make a Mr. Quills?
Would you like to make a Mrs. Quills?
You will need two things to do this.
You will need some clay and some toothpicks.
Shape the clay with your hands.
Make it look something like this:

Now put the toothpicks in the clay.
Your porcupine will look like it is full
of long quills.
Your porcupine can have red quills,
blue quills, brown quills.
You can pick what you like.
After all, this is your porcupine.
There is no other porcupine like the
one you make.
Pick a name for your porcupine.
This is one porcupine you can play with.

30

## Comprehension Check

1. What do porcupines look like?
2. How can a porcupine stop a fight with other animals right away?
3. What do you need to make a play porcupine?
4. What would you do if a porcupine full of quills walked up to you?

# Going Somewhere Special

by Peter Martin Wortmann

Carla found a special book.
The more Carla read this book,
the more Carla wished.

"I want to go somewhere very special,"
she said.
"I must go far from home.
I want to be like the people in
this book.
Here is a girl on skates.
I want to go far from home on skates."

Carla did not take out her skates.
She did not leave her house.
She closed her eyes.
This is what Carla saw.

She had skates on her feet.
She was going all over.
She was very far from home.
She came to a stop in front of some
trees.

Carla opened her eyes.

"That was good," she said.
"But I want to go somewhere much
more special.
I want to go *very* far from home."

Carla read some more in her book.
She read about a train.
So Carla closed her eyes again.
She was on the train!
Carla was in the front of the train.
She could see all over.

Carla opened her eyes.
She was in front of her book.

"That was better," she said.
"But I must go somewhere much more
special.
I want to be on a plane like this one.
It will take me very, very far."

Carla closed her eyes again.
She was on the plane.
She could see that she was very far
from home.
It was a good ride!

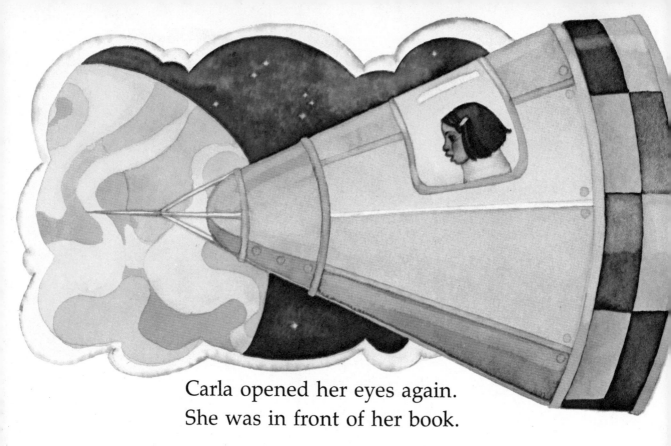

Carla opened her eyes again.
She was in front of her book.

"Where can I go next?" she asked.
"It must be somewhere very, very far away.
I will need to take this special spaceship."

Carla closed her eyes again.
And there was Carla on the special
spaceship!
This time she was very, very far away.

"I like this," said Carla.
"But it is not where I want to be."

36

Carla closed her book.

"I went so far away," she said.
"But I was here all the time."

Carla looked out of her house.
She saw her grandmother's house.

"Now that is very special," Carla said.

At last Carla did know where she wanted
to go.
She ran from her house over to her
grandmother's house.
Carla was very happy to be with her
grandmother.

"I did not know," Carla said, "that
somewhere so special could be here
at home!"

38

## Comprehension Check

1. What things did Carla read about in her book?
2. What did Carla do as she closed her eyes?
3. Did Carla need to go very far?
4. Would you like to go somewhere special? Where would you like to go?

# The Four Know-Littles

a British folk tale
adapted by Michele Spirn

One time there were four Know-Littles.
Boris, Norris, Morris, and Doris.

Know-Littles are funny people.
They do not know very much.
Know-Littles know very little.
They never want to know more.

40

One day Doris, Boris, Morris, and Norris
went for a walk.
They wanted to cut down a tree.

"We will make toothpicks out of it,"
the Know-Littles said.

On the way they saw a porcupine.

"What a pretty dog," said Boris.
"What pretty fur."

Boris went over to see it.
Soon the other Know-Littles were
picking the quills from Boris's hands.

They walked some more.

Doris said, "We must see if all of us
are here.
We were four Know-Littles at the start."

Doris looked at Norris, Boris, and Morris.

"Norris is one, Boris is two, and Morris
is three," she said.
"So there are three of us now.
That is all.
One of us is not here!"

42

All the Know-Littles looked about.

"It must be Morris," said Boris.
"That funny dog took Morris away."

"We will never see Morris again!"
said Morris.

Doris said, "But you are Morris."

"So I am!" said Morris.
"I must be here."

"It is Norris who is not here," said
Morris.
"A special spaceship took her away.
Now she cannot help us cut the tree
into toothpicks!"

"A spaceship took me away," said Norris.

"Who said that?" asked Boris.

"I did," said Norris.

"So you are here," said Boris.

"So I am!" said Norris.

44

"It is Doris who is not here," said Norris.
"She left on the train to see her
grandmother."

"She left!" said three Know-Littles.

"No! No!" said Doris.

"What are you doing here, Doris?" asked
Norris.
"And how is your grandmother?"

Doris said, "I never left."

"You never left?" asked Morris.
"So how are there three of us?"

"It is Boris," said Doris.
"He took the day off to read a book.
It is a book about a fly eating a house."

Boris said, "It is not about a fly."

"Boris, you are here!" said Doris.
"You and Morris and Norris are here.
So who is not?"

46

Mrs. Brown came walking by.
She saw what the Know-Littles were doing.
She wanted to help.

"Doris, Boris, Norris, Morris," she said.
"You are all here.
All four Know-Littles are here."

The Know-Littles looked about.

"Thank you, Mrs. Brown," they said.
"You have found us."

"You were here all the time," said
Mrs. Brown.

"But one of us was not here," said Doris.
"You found Morris."

"No, you found Boris," said Morris.

"No, you found Norris," said Boris.

"No, you found Doris," said Norris.

Mrs. Brown walked away.
"You Know-Littles never want to know!"
she said as she left.

The Know-Littles walked on.
Boris, Norris, Doris, and Morris started
to talk.

"We will find a tree to make toothpicks,"
they said.
"How many of us are here to cut down
the tree?
We will see how many of us are here."

So what went on next?
Who can say?
No one but the Know-Littles know.

**Comprehension Check**
1. What kind of people are Know-Littles?
2. How would you help a Know-Little?

# From A to Z

by Burnham Holmes

Day after day Zota was last.
She was always the last to sit down.
She was always the last to get a book.
She was always at the end of the line.

"I don't like this," Zota said to Betty.
"If I get there on time, I stand around.
If I get there first, I'll be the last.
Why should I always be at the end?"

50

Betty thought about what Zota said.

"I know why it works out that way.
Z is at the very end of the alphabet.
So the last name called out is Zota.
Betty starts with the letter *B*.
So I should be one of the first."

"What should I do?" asked Zota.
"One time I would like to be first
around here."

"Maybe you need a new name," said
Betty.

Zota thought that was funny.

"Names don't grow on trees, you know.
My mother picked the name Zota.
She must have thought it was special.
But maybe I should find a new name.
I'll take any other name."

"Do you want to be first?" asked Betty.

"You can say that again!" said Zota.

"Your name must start with *A*," said Betty.

The next day Zota came to class with a plan.

She said something to the teacher.

After that things were not the same.

Zota was not the last.

She was the first to sit down.

She was the first to get a book.

She was at the front of all the lines.

"This is more like it!" thought Zota.

"You were always the last," said one boy.
"Now I am after you."

"Why are you always first?" asked a girl.

They did not know about Zota's plan.
They did not know what she had said to
the teacher.
They all thought of her as Zota.
Z is at the end.
So Zota should be last.

"How can you be first?" they asked.

Zota laughed and said, "See if you can
find out why!"

54

"Is your name Zota?" asked Betty.

"No, no. Zota is not my name.
But my name is always the same!"

"I don't get this at all," said one girl.

"There is something funny going on,"
said a boy.

The girl with the new name laughed
again.

"Do you know the alphabet?" she asked.
"If you do, you can find my name."

Can *you* find Zota's new name?
What was first is now the end.
What was behind is around in front.
Do you know this around-about name?

Now you know it.
Atoz is Zota's new name.
And that is *A to Z*!

56

## Comprehension Check

1. Why was Zota always at the end of the line?
2. Zota said something to her teacher. What was it?
3. Would you like to pick a new name? What would it be?

# How to Get Warm

by Betty Boegehold

It was one of those very cold days.
Rita and Clay were out walking.

"I am cold," said Rita.
"What will make us warm?"

Clay thought about it.

"I know!" he said.

He began to jump up and down.
So Rita began to jump up and down also.

58

A woman came walking by.
It was Mrs. Ray.
A bunch of plump little yellow
ducklings quacked behind her.
Mrs. Ray saw Rita and Clay jumping.
She began to laugh.

"Why are you two jumping?" she asked.

"To get warm," said Clay.

"I want to get warm also," said Rita,
"but I just can't.
I am just as cold now as I was."

"I can help you," said Mrs. Ray.
"Do you know where my house is?"

"It is the green house next to the park,"
said Rita.

"Take these ducklings down to my house,"
said Mrs. Ray.
"These plump little yellow ducks will
help you get warm, very warm."

"I don't understand," said Rita.

"You will," Mrs. Ray said.
"You will understand very soon."

60

"How can a bunch of yellow ducks make us warm?" Clay asked Mrs. Ray.

"Use your head," she said.
"Just use your head, and you will know also."

Mrs. Ray went away laughing.

"Come on, little ducks," said Rita.
"Run with us.
Run down to the green house."

The little ducks began to run.
But they did not run down to the green house.
The ducklings ran this way and that way.
They ran all over.
Rita and Clay also ran this way and that way.
They ran around and around behind the yellow ducklings.

"Stop, ducks, stop!" called Rita.

62

They all ran by an old house.
Rita saw a big box next to the house.
There was a top on the box.

Rita called to Clay, "We can use
this box.
Just put the ducklings in it!"

She ran after the little ducks.
She picked up one, two, three ducklings.
They went into the box.
Clay picked up four more little ducks.
They also went into the box.

Soon all the ducklings were in the big box
under the big top.

"What a quacking fuss they make," said
Clay.
"We must get this box to the green house
right away.
We must run some more."

"Mrs. Ray was right," laughed Rita.
"These little ducks made me run so much.
Now I am warm, very warm.
But I did not have to use my head.
I just had to use my feet!"

**Comprehension Check**

1. What did Rita and Clay do first to get warm?
2. How did Mrs. Ray help Rita and Clay?

# The Ugly Duckling

by Hans Christian Andersen
adapted by Barbara Sobel

One time a dog, a porcupine, and a
bunch of ducks lived in the woods.
They had a good time together.
But there was one duckling that did
not have a good time.
He was not like the other ducks.
He was little and funny-looking.
The other animals thought he was ugly.

The dog thought, "I am good-looking.
I am big and brown.
But you, little duck, you are ugly!"
So the dog ran away from the duckling.

The porcupine thought, "I am pretty
and full of sharp quills.
I am something special.
But you, duckling, good-by!"
And she just walked away.

The other ducks thought, "We have
plump shapes.
You look like a toothpick next to us."
The ducks quacked at the little one.

The animals played all day.
The dog ran around.
The porcupine sat in her tree.
The ducks jumped in and out of
the water.
But they would not play with the ugly
duckling.

"Why are you doing this to me?" asked
the ugly duckling.

The other animals said, "You look funny.
So we don't like you."

The little duckling said he would run
away.

"Good!" said the dog.

The porcupine said, "Don't write me
any letters."

The other ducks quacked, "So long."

So the ugly duckling left the woods.
For a long time, he went from here
to there and from there to here.
The duckling was not happy.
But there was something he did not
know.
He was growing all the time.
He was growing into a very pretty
bird.
But no one told him this.

70

One day the ugly duckling came back to the woods.

He saw the dog, the porcupine, and the ducks.

They were just the same.

The dog was just as big and brown and good-looking.

The porcupine was just as pretty.

The ducks had the same plump shapes.

But the ugly duckling was not the
same at all.
The other animals did not know him.

"Who is that pretty bird?" asked the
porcupine with the sharp quills.
"He is good-looking!"

"He is so tall," said the dog.
"He is a very pretty bird."

"He also has a plump shape!" quacked
the ducks.
"He is something special!"

"Don't you know me?" asked the very pretty, tall bird.
"I am the ugly duckling."

"You did not want me," he said to the ducks.

"You ran away from me," he said to the dog.

"You told me not to write any letters," he said to the porcupine.

"That was not good," said the animals.
"Now we know.
All animals are special.
We should not make any animal go away.
Will you live in the woods with us?"

The tall bird said he would.
So the animals lived together again.
This time they were all happy.

**Comprehension Check**

1. Why did the ugly duckling run away?
2. Will the tall bird be happy in the
   woods? Why or why not?

74

# The Ducks

by Alice Wilkins

When our ducks waddle to the pond,
They're as awkward as awkward can be—
But when they get in the water and swim,
They glide most gracefully.

75

# Weather People

by Christine Economos

What will today be like?
Will the air be cold or warm?
Will it be stormy?
Will there be much wind or just a little?
Will rain fall?
Will it be too cold to play outside?

There are people who can find out these
things.
These people find out about the weather.

76

There are many people working in
this room.
They are finding out about the weather.
A number of things help these people
find out about the weather.

This woman uses a thermometer.
She can find out if the air outside
is warm or cold.
There are numbers on the thermometer.
The woman reads the numbers.
There is a red line on the thermometer.
If the red line goes to a high
number, it is warmer.
If the red line goes to a low
number, it is colder.
The red line is going to a low number.
The woman reads the numbers on the
thermometer.
She knows it will be a very cold day.

78

This is a weather balloon.
The balloon is outside.
It is working way up in the air.
The weather balloon finds out about
the wind.
It finds out if it will be stormy.

How can the balloon do this?
It finds out how cold or warm the air is.
The people in the weather room write
down what the balloon finds out.

This woman works with a big map
almost all the time.
She can see if it will be stormy.
She knows where the rain began.
She knows where it goes next.

"Will rain fall today?" asks one man.

"It will rain," says the woman.
"It will rain almost all day.
Look outside."

The man goes to look outside.
The rain has started to fall.

All the weather people in this room
work together now.
They write down what they know.
They know it will be very stormy.
There will be wind and rain.
The red line on the thermometer
will be at a low number.

People will need to know about the
weather today.
How can they find out about it?
They can find out from the weather
people.

"It will be very stormy," the man says.
"It will rain almost all day.
There will be very cold winds.
It is going to be the coldest day in
a long time.
Put on your warmest things if you go
outside.
Thank you.
And see you again soon."

82

## Comprehension Check

1. What do people need to know about the weather?
2. How do thermometers work?
3. What do weather balloons find out?
4. How do you find out about the weather?

# Three Nights of Magic

by Michele Spirn

Once there was a pretty house.
Mr. and Mrs. Green and Pat and Sue
lived in the house.
But the Greens were not happy.

"Things are always the same around
here," said Mrs. Green.

"All the days are the same in this
house," said Pat.

"We need something new around here,"
they all said.

84

Little did the Greens know.
Some elves were in their pretty house.
That night the elves got together
to do their magic.

They said, "We might, we might, we might
make people big this night."

While the night became day, the Greens
became very large.

Sue was the first to get up.
She was almost as large as her room!
She became taller and taller.

"Pat, come here!" called Sue.

"I can't," said Pat.
"My head is almost over the top of the house!
I can't get my large feet into my shoes."

Mr. Green was as tall as the trees.
Mrs. Green was taller.
The Greens became such large people that
they had to go outside.
They did not like it at all.
So they wished to be smaller.

86

That night it rained and rained.
It was such a stormy night that
no one wanted to be outside.
But the Greens were too large to be
in their house.
They were outside while it rained.

Once again the elves got together.
"We might, we might, we might make
people small this night."

While night became day, the
Greens became smaller and smaller.

The Greens never thought they could become such small people.
They became too small.
Mrs. Green could sit on an orange.
Mr. Green was as tall as a toothpick.
A large rabbit jumped over Mr. Green while he was walking outside.
The rabbit thought Mr. Green was such a funny little thing!

The Greens did not want to be so small.
Once again they wished.
This time they wished to be as they
once were.

The elves got together.
But they did not want to do any magic.

"These people are always wishing,"
said one elf.
"Large. Small. Same. I say good night!"

But one elf wanted to help.

"Don't make such a fuss," said this one.

So once more the elves got together.
"We might, we might, we might make
people as they first were this night."

While night became day, the Greens
became as they first were.
Once more they were not too large and
not too small.

"It is the same around here once again,"
said the Greens.
"And it is a good thing!"

## Comprehension Check

1. Why were the Greens not happy?
2. What did the magic do?
3. Would you like to be smaller or
   taller? Why?

# WHAT A DAY!

by Duncan Searl

"Pam. Pam! PAM!"
Father had already called three times.
But Pam wanted to sleep even more.

"Get up," said Father.

"Why can't I sleep?" asked Pam.

"You can't sleep because you are
already late," said Father.
"You are in the school show today."

92

Pam jumped up.
The school show was today!
The show was a play about animals in
the woods.
Pam was the porcupine.
She could not be late for the show.

"Slow down and eat your breakfast,"
said Father.

"I don't have time to eat it all,"
said Pam.

The school bus was already at the
bus stop.
Pam ran as fast as she could.
Pam ran right into Mrs. Rienza!
She ran into Mrs. Rienza's oranges too.

"Look what you did!" said Mrs. Rienza.
The woman's oranges were all over.

"I'll help you get the oranges,"
said Pam.

Pam found the last orange.
She looked up.
The bus had already left.

"I missed the bus because I helped
Mrs. Rienza," Pam thought.
"I helped her because I ran into her.
I ran into her because I was late.
I was late because I like to sleep.
And now I have to walk to school."

It was a long way to the school.
Pam walked as fast as she could.
She even ran some of the way.
After a while Pam saw a little boy.
The boy was calling to a cat in a tree.

"My cat will not come down," the
boy said.

"Maybe I can get it," said Pam.

96

While Pam was up in the tree, a big red
truck pulled up.
It was the firefighters!

"We got a call about a cat in a tree,"
one firefighter said.
"But all I see is a funny porcupine."

"I have the cat," Pam called down.

"Good," said the firefighter.
"But why are you not in school?"

So Pam told the firefighter all
about that day.
She told the firefighter why she
was late.
Pam even told him about the school
show.

"The show must go on!" said the
firefighter.
"Jump in the truck.
We will give you a ride."

Soon Pam was at school.
She got there just as the bus did.

"The show will go on!" she called to her teacher.
"And it is not even late!"

**Comprehension Check**

1. Why did Pam want to be on time for school?
2. Why was Pam almost late for school?
3. Pam helped the boy get his cat. How did this help Pam get to school on time?

# The Elves and the Shoes

by the Brothers Grimm
adapted by Rhoda Goldstein

Once upon a time a man and a woman lived
in a little old house.
They worked and worked all day.
The man would stand at his table and make
shoes.
First he made lines on the leather.
Next he cut out the shapes and made new
shoes.
The woman would show the shoes to people.
But not many people came in to buy.

100

One day the woman said, "We work
and work.
But we don't even have things to eat.
We are cold.
But we don't have sweaters to put on."

The man put his hands over his eyes.

"I know," he said.
"We need so many things.
But more people must buy these shoes."

One night they worked very late.
There was not much light in the room.

"It is already time to go to sleep," said
the woman.

The man looked at his table.
There was very little on it.
There was just some leather for two
more shoes.

"First I want to cut out these last two
shapes," he said.

The man worked as fast as he could.
He picked up the shapes and said, "After I make these into shoes, I will have no more leather.
What will I do?"

He put the shapes down and walked out of the room.
There was not a sound in the house.
But that night there would be magic at his work table.

Two elves came into the room.
They were very small and funny.
Up they jumped on the table.
They picked up the leather shapes.
Their little hands began to work.
Soon they looked down and laughed.
There were two new shoes!

"We come and we go," they called.
And they were off.

The next day the man saw the shoes.

"Look here," he said to the woman.
"I could never find better shoes.
Who could have made these for us?"

Just then a girl came in.

"How pretty!" she said.
"I would like to buy these shoes."
So the girl took the shoes.

"Now we can buy more leather," said
the woman.
She went to buy leather for four shoes.

It was already very late that night.
But the man made lines on the leather.
Next he cut out four shapes.
He went to sleep.

Again the elves came into the room.
Again their little hands began to work.
There were four new shoes!
The elves laughed together.

They called, "We come and we go."
And they were off.

The next day a number of people
came in.
They wanted to buy the new shoes.
The man and the woman were happy because
now they could buy leather for eight shoes.

Things began to get even better.
More and more people wanted shoes.
The man made more and more shapes.
The elves came night after night.
They always made the shapes into shoes.

One night the woman and the man
wanted to see what went on.
It was very late.
They made no sound at all.
They looked into the workroom.
There they saw the elves on the table.

"They are so good to us," thought the man
and the woman.
"We should make something for these two
elves."

So they made two pretty little sweaters.

The next night they put out the sweaters.
Soon the elves came.
The elves put on the sweaters.

"Thank you," they called into the air.
They laughed and ran away.
They never came again.

The two people began to laugh also.

"You helped us get the things we
needed," they called.
"So we thank you too!"

Comprehension Check
1. How did the man make shoes?
2. What would shoes made by an elf
   look like?

# Out of the Oven

by W. Martin Young

Can you tell what these people do?
They get up before almost all of us.
They are on their way to work before it is
even light outside.
They know they cannot be late.
These are very special people.
They make something that many of us eat.

110

Can you tell what these people do?
Yes! They are bakers.
They all work together in this bakery.
In this bakery they all bake bread.

We buy just one or two or three loaves
of bread.
But these people must bake enough for
all of us.
The bakers must bake a large number
of loaves.

How do the bakers bake enough for all of us?

Just look at how big their ovens are.

Look at how many ovens they have.

There is bread in the ovens all day long.

First the bakers shape the bread.

They put the loaves in the ovens.

They shape other loaves before the first ones come out.

The first loaves come out of the ovens, and the next loaves go in.

These bakers are very good at their work.
But even they cannot always tell how
much bread will be enough.
Some people come into the bakery late
in the day.
They ask for one kind of bread.
The bakers must tell these people that
there is no more.

"We cannot give you what you want today,"
the bakers say.
"But come back again."

Bakers can also bake special breads.
They shape the loaves in special ways
before the loaves go into the ovens.
The bakers can make bread in the shapes
of animals and in the shapes of alphabet
letters.
They work a long time to shape these
breads.
But they know the breads will make
people happy.
Even if you ask for a funny shape, some
bakers will say, "Yes, I can make that
for you."

The bakers who come to work first cannot work all day and all night.
Other bakers come in to take over the work.
These other bakers must work late at night to bake enough bread.
Working late is something almost all bakers do once in a while.

The bakers must do one last thing before
they go home.
They must clean the bakery.
They cannot leave before they have
cleaned.
The bakers clean the ovens.
They clean all the things they use.

116

The bakers look all around.

"Yes, we have cleaned it all," they say.

"Yes, it was a long day.

But now it is time to go home."

## Comprehension Check

1. How do bakers bake bread?
2. Why do bakers start work before it is light outside?
3. Would you like to bake something? How would you do it?

# How Can This Be?

by Duncan Searl and Wendy Ableman

Hector was moving into a new house.
He was sure he would like the house.
Its rooms were big.
There were trees around the house.

Hector helped carry some boxes from the
moving truck.
He saw a girl next to the truck.

"I can carry these boxes by myself,"
said Hector.

"I could carry these boxes by myself too," said
the girl.
"But why don't we carry them together?"

118

Hector asked the girl, "Who are you?"

"I am your neighbor," she said.
"I live in the green house over there."

The girl told Hector all about their
school and their neighbors.

"You are sure to like our school,"
she said.
"Its teachers are the best.
Our neighbors here are great too."

The girl helped Hector carry things
from the truck.
Hector was sure he would like his new
neighbor and his new house.

After a while the girl went home.
Hector helped carry some other things.
There was a box of shoes, a bunch of
sweaters, and two tables.

Hector started to carry a table.

"I could carry our other things by
myself," he said.
"But I cannot carry these tables by myself."

"Just don't ask me to help!" said a girl.
"I will not carry them with you.
And I will not carry them by myself."
It was Hector's new neighbor again.
But this time she did not look so happy.

"Are you sure you want to move here?"
the girl asked.
"Our school and its teachers are not
very good.
Its rooms are not even clean enough.
I am sure you will not like our school."

Hector looked at the girl.
"But you just said the school and its
teachers were the best," he said to her.

"The houses around here are ugly," said
the girl.
"And our neighbors are not home enough.
You will not like them.
*I* always play by myself."

With that, the girl walked away.

Hector could not understand why the
girl said such things.
What had become of the best school?
What had become of its teachers?
What had become of the great neighbors?

"What has become of that funny girl?"
asked Hector.
"And what will become of me in this
new house?"

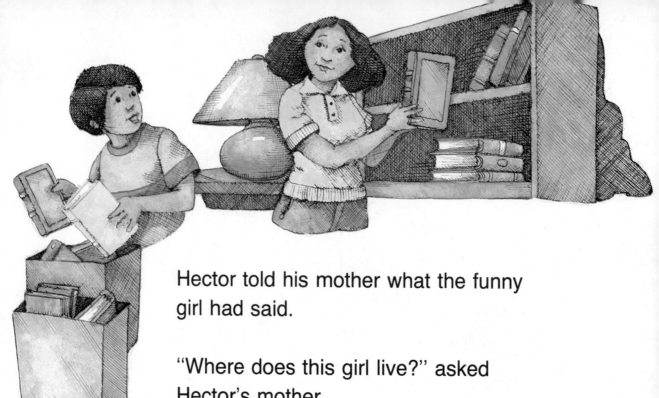

Hector told his mother what the funny girl had said.

"Where does this girl live?" asked Hector's mother.

"She lives in the green house," he said.

"Yes, I know who lives in that house," said Hector's mother.
She laughed.
"Go over to the green house, Hector. You will find out what has become of that funny girl."

Hector went over to the green house.
He saw two girls playing under a tree.
The two of them looked just the same!

"Hector," called the girls, "we are twins.
We wanted to have some twin fun for
just a little while.
We were sure you would find out soon.
We think it is great to have a new neighbor."

Hector laughed.
"Yes, one new neighbor is good," he said.
"But twin neighbors are even better!"

**Comprehension Check**
1. What did the first girl tell Hector
   about the school and the neighbors?
2. What did the other girl tell Hector?
3. What did Hector find out at the end?

# Clouds

by Arnold Lobel

A little mouse went for a walk with
his mother.
They went to the top of a hill and
looked at the sky.

"Look!" said Mother.
"We can see pictures in the clouds."

The little mouse and his mother saw
many pictures in the clouds.

They saw a castle, a rabbit, a mouse.

"I am going to pick flowers,"
said Mother.

"I will stay here and watch the clouds,"
said the little mouse.

The little mouse saw a big cloud in
the sky.
It grew bigger and bigger.

The cloud became a cat.
The cat came nearer and nearer to
the little mouse.

"Help!" shouted the little mouse,
and he ran to his mother.
"There is a big cat in the sky!"
cried the little mouse.
"I am afraid."

128

Mother looked up at the sky.

"Do not be afraid," she said.
"See, the cat has turned back into
a cloud again."

The little mouse saw that this was
true, and he felt better.
He helped his mother pick flowers,
but he did not look up at the sky
for the rest of the afternoon.

# The Mouse and the Winds

by Arnold Lobel

A mouse went out in his boat, but
there was no wind.
The boat did not move.

"Wind!" shouted the mouse.
"Come down and blow my boat across
the lake."

"Here I am," said the west wind.

The west wind blew and blew.
The mouse and the boat went up in
the air and landed on the roof of
a house.

"Wind!" shouted the mouse.
"Come down and blow my boat off
this house!"

"Here I am," said the east wind.

The east wind blew and blew.
The mouse and the boat and the house
went up in the air and landed on the
top of a tree.

"Wind!" shouted the mouse.
"Come down and blow my boat off this
house and off this tree!"

"Here I am," said the south wind.

The south wind blew and blew.
The mouse and the boat and the house
and the tree went up in the air
and landed on top of a mountain.

"Wind!" shouted the mouse.
"Come down and blow my boat off this house and off this tree and off this mountain!"

"Here I am," said the north wind.

The north wind blew and blew.
The mouse and the boat and the house and the tree and the mountain went up in the air . . . and came down into the lake.

The mountain sank and became an island.
The tree landed on the island and burst
into bloom.
The house landed next to the tree.

A lady looked out of a window in
the house and said, "What a nice
place to live!"

And the mouse just sailed away.

# SECTION TWO

# Who Will Fill Up the Little House?

an Eastern European folk tale
adapted by Betty Boegehold

One time a man and a woman had
three boys.
They called their boys Joe, Jake,
and Jon.
For a long time all five people lived
together in the same little house.
But this house was too small for so
many people.

One day Joe said, "I am too big to live here.
I must find a new house to live in."

"I am very big now too," said Jake.
"I must also find a new house."

Jon said, "I want to go away.
I am big and old enough now too."

"Yes," said the man.
"You all must go off and make new homes."

"Hold on!" said the woman.
"I have a little house in the woods.
One of you can live there."

"Can I live there?" asked Joe.

"No, I want to live there," said Jake.

Jon said, "But I want to live there too."

"Who will get your house?" the man asked.

The woman thought and thought.
At last she said, "I know what to do!
Yes, I will give my house to the boy who
fills it up to the top.
The one who fills it with any kind of
thing at all can live in my house!"

"I will go first," said Joe.
"I will fill your little house all up.
Give me just one day and you will see."

The next day they all went to see the little house.

The man said, "I see boxes, a large number of old boxes."

"I see many old shoes," said Jake.

"And I see old tables," Jon said.

The woman said, "But the house is not filled to the top.
So you cannot live here, Joe."

"I can fill up the house," said Jake.
"Soon you will see it all filled up!"

So the next day they went to the house.

"I see a number of stones," said the man.

"I see bunches of letters," said Joe.

"I see porcupine quills," said Jon.
"Porcupine quills are here and there."

"I don't see very many things at all,"
said the woman.
"Jake, you cannot live here."

"But I will live here," said Jon.
"This very night I will fill up the
little house."

"No, no," said Joe.
"If I could not fill up the little
house, you will not fill it up."

"I know you can't do it," said Jake.

"Just come and see," said Jon.

That night the man, the woman, Joe,
and Jake came to the house.

"I can't see much at all," said
the man.

"We cannot see a thing," said Joe
and Jake.

The woman called, "Jon, where
are you?
How can we see if you have filled
the house?"

"Come next to the house," Jon said.
"Come here and you will see."

The man, the woman, and the two boys
went next to the house.
But they could not see a thing.

"Now look!" called Jon.
"See how I am going to fill the house!"

He did something with his hand.

144

They all looked.
The house was filled with light!
Up and down and all around, there was
warm yellow light!

"Have I filled up your little house now?"
Jon asked his mother.

His mother laughed.
"Yes, you have," she said.
"You filled it all up with light.
So now you can live in it."

And that is just what Jon did.

## Comprehension Check

1. Why did the boys want to leave
   their first house?
2. What things did Joe and Jake put
   in the little house in the woods?
3. Did you like what Jon did to fill
   the house? Why or why not?

# Light

by Debra Berkowitz

Warm light
Sun on my arm.
Night light
Keeps me from harm.
Bright light
Sun on the snow.
Fire light
Just a warm glow.
Pink light
First blush of day.
Moon light
Showing the way.

Warm, pink, bright
Fire, moon, night.
        Light.

# At Home on the Ranch

by Harrison Hawkins

What do you think a ranch is like today?
It is not very much like the ranches in
the old cowboy shows on TV.

There are cowboys on the ranch today.
There are cowgirls too.
Cowboys and cowgirls are called *ranch hands*.

Many ranch hands have horses today.
But they use trucks just as much as
they use horses.

The main work of the old-time ranch hand
was looking after the cattle.
Cattle need hay and good water.
The old-time ranch hand let the cattle move
across the ranch to find these things.

Today ranch hands look after cattle.
But they don't do it the same way.
They let the cattle stay where they are.
They carry hay to the cattle in trucks.

148

The old-time cowboy let the cattle run all
across the ranch.
Today there are many trucks on the roads.
The cattle could get hurt.
So today ranch hands make their cattle stay
behind fences.
They must make sure all the fences and
roads are in good shape.

On many days ranch hands start work
before breakfast.
They ride out across the ranch.
One of them will make a fire.
He makes breakfast while the others work
with the cattle.

"Come and get it!" he calls.

The ranch hands are happy to stop working
and have breakfast.
They think eating outside is great.

150

Ranch people do not like cold, stormy
weather.
Old-time ranch hands just had to sit out the
stormy weather.
They could not get to their cattle.
The cattle did not have enough to eat.

Today ranch hands can use planes to get hay
to their cattle.
They can move across the ranch even if the
roads are washed out.

The best time on a ranch is roundup time.
The old-time cowboys would ride across the
ranch looking for cattle.
It took days and days for the roundup.
Some cattle would always get away.
The cowboys would ride after them.
They would lasso the ones that ran off.

Today ranch people know how to lasso too.
But not many cattle get away.
They stay all together behind the fences.

*Skills Unit 10*

Old-time ranch hands would move the
cattle down the trail after the roundup.
One would call, "Move them out!"

The cattle would start down the road.
The ranch hands would ride their horses.
But it was a long walk for the cattle.

Today ranch people carry their cattle in
trucks or trains.
The cattle don't walk the long trail.

A ranch is not all work and no play.
Work comes first.
But the people on a ranch have good times
after their work is over.
They like to sit around a fire at night.
They eat and show off with the lasso.
They sing and think about the old-time
cowboys.

Comprehension Check

1. How do ranch hands look after cattle
   today?
2. Why did old-time ranch hands
   not like stormy weather?
3. Do you think you might like to live on
   a ranch? Why or why not?

154

# My Own Foal

by Marge Blaine

This is Winona.
She was just born.
She was the smallest of all the foals.
But she was my own.

Each of the foals would stay with its
own mother in the stable.
I would give each mother some oats and
hay to eat.

Winona began to grow little by little.
I went to see her each day.
And each day she was able to do
something new.

Soon Winona was able to run.
She was able to eat her own oats.
She began to play with the other foals.

I took Winona to the woods each day.
She wanted to roam among the trees.
After a while she was able to run very
fast among the trees.

Winona was able to do many things.
But she did not grow very big.
She was always the smallest foal.
For me, she was also the most special.

This is my neighbor Lanu.
He liked to boast about his own foal.
Lanu did not think Winona was very special.
He always said Winona was just too small.
Lanu did not think my foal could do much.

Winona would come to me each time
I called.
I wanted to show this to Lanu.
So we went to the stable one day.
I called Winona but she would not
come to me.

Lanu said again that my foal could not
do much.
But I had a plan.
I would show Lanu what my own foal
was able to do.

The next day Lanu and I took all the
foals out of the stable.
We walked them to the road.
We wanted to see which one could run
the fastest.

It had rained the night before.
The road was very slick.
But I was sure Winona could run fast
even on that slick road.
"Run, Winona. Run," I called.

160

Winona and the other foals began to run.
Each one ran as fast as it could.
But my own was the fastest.

Winona ran faster than the other foals.
She ran even faster than she had run
among the trees.
And she ran much faster than Lanu and I did!

Lanu said to me, "You don't need to boast about Winona now. I *know* she is special."

That is just what I had thought all the time!

## Comprehension Check

1. What things did Winona like to do?
2. Why did the girl think Winona was special?

# Jomo Says Something Special

an African folk tale
adapted by Barbara Sobel

Once upon a time there was a man
called Jomo.
Jomo had left his home to see faraway
things and new people.
At last it was time for Jomo to go home.
He walked and walked for many days.

One day he saw some houses and some
people.

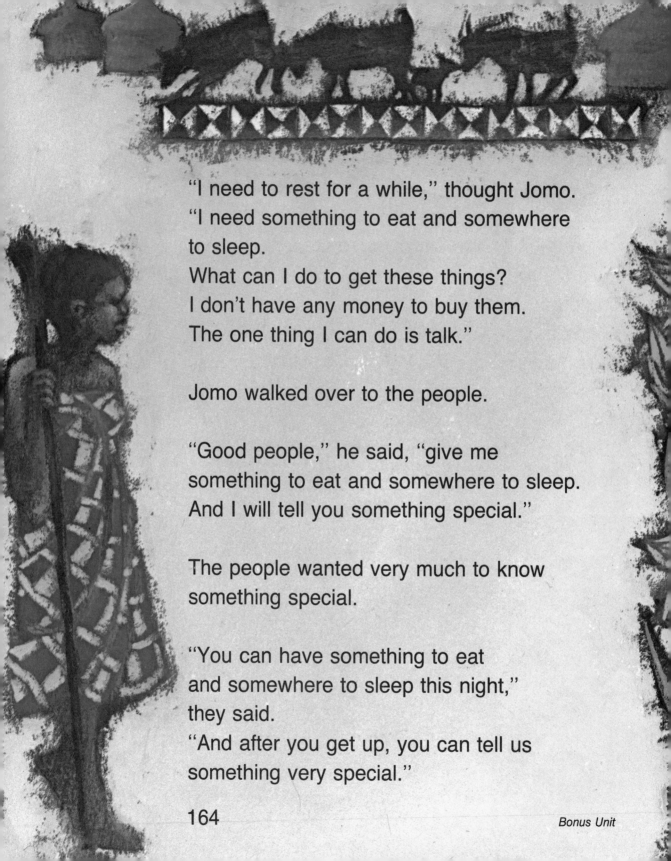

"I need to rest for a while," thought Jomo.
"I need something to eat and somewhere
to sleep.
What can I do to get these things?
I don't have any money to buy them.
The one thing I can do is talk."

Jomo walked over to the people.

"Good people," he said, "give me
something to eat and somewhere to sleep.
And I will tell you something special."

The people wanted very much to know
something special.

"You can have something to eat
and somewhere to sleep this night,"
they said.
"And after you get up, you can tell us
something very special."

164

One woman gave Jomo something to eat.
One man took Jomo to his house to sleep.

The next day Jomo got up.
The people were already in front of
the house.
Jomo went outside.
He had a good plan.

"Good people," said Jomo, "do you know
what I am going to say to you?"

The people looked at each other.

"No, we do not know," they said.

"How can I talk to you?" asked Jomo.
"You do not know even the smallest thing
about what I will say.
Go home and think about it for one day."

So all the people went home.
A woman gave Jomo something to eat.
A man took Jomo home to sleep.
Jomo was able to rest for one more day.

166

The next day the people got together.
They thought about what to do.
They wanted Jomo to tell them something
very special.
So they made their own plan.

Jomo got up and went outside.
Again he said, "Good people, do you
know what I am going to say?"

This time all the people said, "Yes."

Jomo said, "You already know.
So why should I tell you what you
already know?
Go home and think about this again."

The people went home to think.
And Jomo could rest for one more day.

The people came together to talk.
They talked about what Jomo ate day after
day.
They talked about Jomo sleeping in their
homes each night.
So far Jomo had not told them even one thing.
The people thought about what to do.
They came up with a new plan.

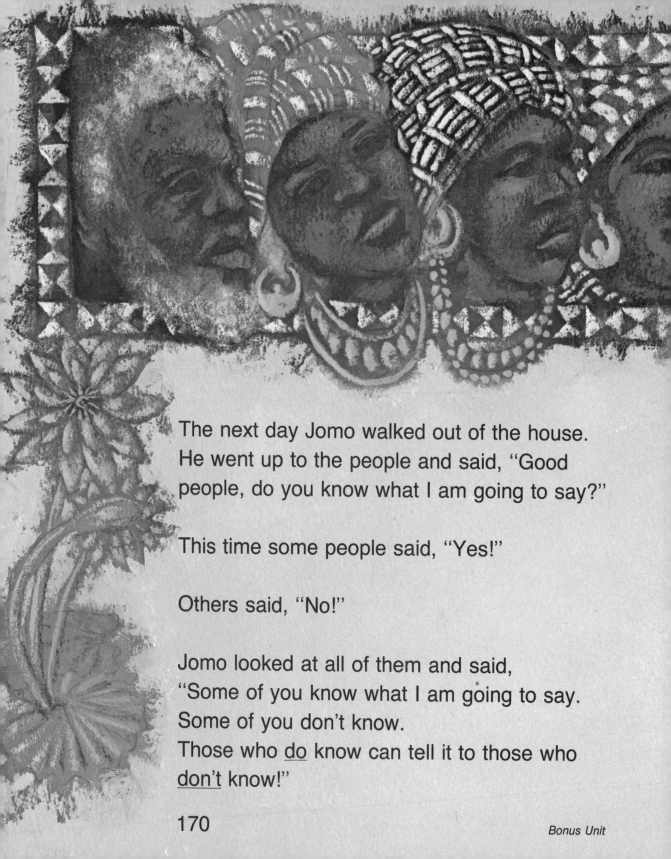

The next day Jomo walked out of the house. He went up to the people and said, "Good people, do you know what I am going to say?"

This time some people said, "Yes!"

Others said, "No!"

Jomo looked at all of them and said, "Some of you know what I am going to say. Some of you don't know. Those who <u>do</u> know can tell it to those who <u>don't</u> know!"

170

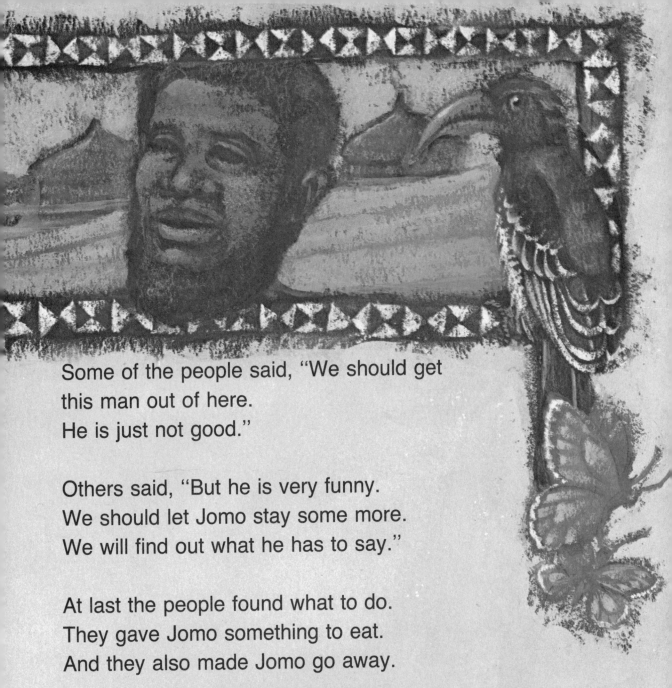

Some of the people said, "We should get
this man out of here.
He is just not good."

Others said, "But he is very funny.
We should let Jomo stay some more.
We will find out what he has to say."

At last the people found what to do.
They gave Jomo something to eat.
And they also made Jomo go away.

"Enough is enough," said the people.
"What Jomo has to say could not be so
special."

Jomo walked down the road.

"This could not be better," he said.
"I have something to eat for now.
And by night I will be home!"

## Comprehension Check

1. Why did Jomo stop to talk to the people?
2. Why did the people let Jomo stay with them?
3. Did you think Jomo was funny? Why or why not?

172

# Funny Mr. Dee

by Anthony Graham

Mr. Dee and Mrs. Dee lived together in
a small house under a tree.
But Mr. Dee always said, "We live in a
*big* house *over* a tree."

"That is how Mr. Dee does it," said
Mrs. Dee.
"If I say close the door, he opens the door.
If I say there are too many animals in
the house, he says there are too few.
Back to front and front to back.
That is how Mr. Dee still does it!"

One day Mr. Dee was about to go out.

"It is raining," said Mrs. Dee.
"Take a raincoat with you."

"See you soon," called Mr. Dee as he
walked out the door without a raincoat.
He walked out the door without a raincoat,
without a sweater, without anything
warm on.

Mrs. Dee said, "Back to front and front to
back.
That is how Mr. Dee still does it!"

174

Mr. Dee went for a long walk.
On his way he saw his neighbor Sue.

"Mr. Dee," said Sue, "why are you
walking around without a raincoat?
You look cold.
Come to our house for something warm
to drink."

"I am cold," said Mr. Dee.
"So I don't want anything warm to drink."

"Back to front, front to back," said Sue.
"That is how Mr. Dee still does it!"

Mr. Dee went walking in the woods among the trees.
Soon he did not know where he was.

"I don't see anything I know," said Mr. Dee.
"I don't see anything but all these trees and a few big stones."

176

Mr. Dee saw a boy walking in the woods.

"Can you help me?" asked Mr. Dee.
"Can you tell me how to get home?"

"Where do you live?" asked the boy.

"I live in the red house behind the
school," said Mr. Dee.

"See that yellow tree?" asked the boy.
"Go to the right at the yellow tree.
The trail there will take you back home."

Mr. Dee walked over to the yellow tree.
Did he go to the right?
No, he went to the left.

Mr. Dee walked and walked.

"I still don't see anything I know,"
he said.
"I don't see anything but the woods.
I might always be in these woods!
Maybe I will go back to the yellow tree.
Maybe I should do what the boy said."

Mr. Dee went back to the yellow tree.
He found the trail.
The trail took Mr. Dee across a few
roads, over a few big stones, and under
a few large trees.
At last Mr. Dee was at his own door.

Mrs. Dee saw Mr. Dee and said, "My, my,
you are back home at last.
Come inside the door."

So Mr. Dee walked inside.

Mrs. Dee asked, "Don't you want to go out for a long walk again?"

Mr. Dee just laughed.
"I think I have done enough walking for a while," he said.
"I'll stay around here for a few days."

"My, my," said Mrs. Dee, "you are not the same!
Front to front and back to back.
That is how Mr. Dee does it now."

**Comprehension Check**
1. Mr. Dee was a funny man. What did he do that was funny?
2. Why did Mr. Dee go back to the yellow tree?
3. What would Mr. Dee do if it were very warm outside?

# On Stage

by Burton Byrd

One day Mrs. Hart said to her class,
"Who can tell me what a play is?"

Only Kim put her hand in the air.

"We all get up on stage and say some
things," Kim said.

"That is right, Kim," said Mrs. Hart.
"But there are many things we must do
before we are ready to get up on stage."

Then Mrs. Hart said, "There is one very
good way for us to find out about a play.
We will put on our own play.
We must start by picking out the play
that we want to do."

"The one I like best," said Mark, "is
The Turtle and the Rabbit."

"I like that one too," said many children
in the class.

182

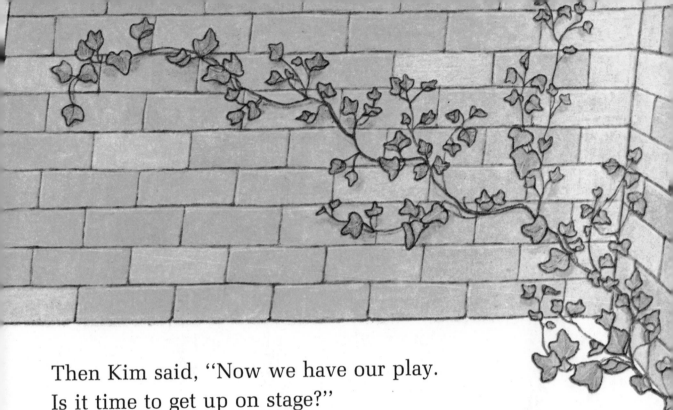

Then Kim said, "Now we have our play.
Is it time to get up on stage?"

"No," said Mrs. Hart, "first we must all
know what goes on in this play.
Then we can find out which part each of
us will take."

Mrs. Hart read the play to the class.

"I want to be the rabbit," said Ann.

"I want to be the duck," said Mark.

"I want to be the horse," said Lee.

Mrs. Hart said, "We also need a dog,
a fly, and a turtle."

The children picked their parts.
Kim took the part of the turtle.
Then Kim said, "Now we know who will
play each part.
Are we ready to get up on stage now?"

"Not so soon," said Mrs. Hart.
"We know who will play each part.
But this is not the only thing we must
know."

184

"Each of you," said Mrs. Hart, "must know what words to say.
The better you know your words, the better our play will be."

So the children read their words over and over.
Then they were ready to say their words to each other.
They did the play just as they would do it on stage.
They did the play a few times.

"Now we all know what words to say,"
said Kim.
"Is it time to get up on stage?"

"There is only one thing we must do now,"
said Mrs. Hart.
"We must make our costumes."

All that day the children worked only
on their costumes.
Some of the costumes were very pretty.
Some of them were also very funny.
Then at last it was time to get up
on stage.

186

The children in Mrs. Hart's class put on
*The Turtle and the Rabbit.*
Some boys and girls from other classes
came to see it.
They all liked the play very much.
This made Kim very happy.
She thought about all the things that
made the play so good.

"First we picked a play," said Kim.
"Then we all picked our parts.
Then we said our words just as we would
on stage.
Next we made costumes.
And only then was everything ready.
There is one thing I know now.
There is more to a play than saying
words on stage!"

**Comprehension Check**

1. What things did the class do to put on
   the play?
2. Tell about a play you would like to
   put on.

188

# The Turtle and the Rabbit

a fable by Aesop
adapted by W. Martin Young

(*TURTLE* is on stage. *RABBIT* runs
on.)

RABBIT: Where are you going?

TURTLE: I am going to get a drink of
water just outside the woods.

RABBIT: That is where I am going too.
It is a long way from here.
I will get there very soon because
I am so fast.
But you will not get there for days.

TURTLE: Say what you wish, Mr. Rabbit.
I will get there all the same.

RABBIT: I never thought anything could
   be as slow as you.
   Why, you are as slow as a turtle!

TURTLE: I am a turtle, Mr. Rabbit.
   And I just might find my way out of
   these woods before you do.

RABBIT: You make me laugh.
   I am going to run off now.
   We will see who takes the first drink.

TURTLE: The one who runs off first does
   not always laugh last, Mr. Rabbit.

RABBIT (runs *for a while and then stops*):
> I like to run.
> But who needs all this work!
> What I need is a little sleep.
> That turtle is still far behind me.
> I will be up and on my way even
> before he comes by.
>
> (RABBIT sits down and goes to sleep.)

(*TURTLE* is on stage. *DUCK* walks on.)

DUCK: Where are you going?

TURTLE: I am going to get a drink.

DUCK: Me too.
But you will never get there if you walk like that.
Why don't you fly there like me?

TURTLE: Do I look like a duck to you?
No, I look like a turtle.
I walk like a turtle because I *am* a turtle.
And we turtles like being slow.

DUCK: If you say so, Mr. Turtle.

192

(*DUCK walks off stage. CAT walks on.*)

CAT: Where are you going?

TURTLE: I am going to get some water.

CAT: I don't even like to drink water.

TURTLE: I never said that you did.

CAT: Why don't you come and play with me?

TURTLE: I don't have time to play.

CAT: I wish you were not so slow. Then you would have time.

(*CAT walks off stage. HORSE walks
on.*)

HORSE: Where are you going?

TURTLE: I am going to get a drink.

HORSE: That is where I am going too.
Why don't you jump on my back?
We will be there in no time at all.

TURTLE: Turtles do not jump.
And we do not wish to do anything
fast.

HORSE: If you say so, Mr. Turtle.

194

(*HORSE* walks off stage. *DOG* walks on.)

DOG: Where are you going?

TURTLE: I am going to get some water.

DOG: Water? Who wants water?
Why not come with me and run
after some people and bark?

TURTLE: I do not bark, Mr. Dog.
And I do not run after people.

DOG: What do you like to do?

TURTLE: I only like being a turtle.

(*DOG walks off stage. FLY walks on.*)

TURTLE: Good day, Mrs. Fly.

I am going to get a drink.

Why don't you come with me?

(*They walk some more and find
RABBIT, HORSE,* and *DUCK sleeping.*)

TURTLE: Just look at them!

FLY: They look so nice, sleeping the
day away.

Why don't you stop and sleep too?

TURTLE: I have other things to do.

We turtles are slow but sure.

I would not be a turtle if I let
myself stop.

196

(*TURTLE* and *FLY* walk to the water.
They drink it.
Then *RABBIT, HORSE,* and *DUCK* get
up and run to the water.)

RABBIT, HORSE, and DUCK together: How
    can this be?
    How could you get here first?

TURTLE: I am a turtle, you know.

RABBIT, HORSE, DUCK: A very slow turtle.

TURTLE: Yes, I am slow.
    But I am also very sure.
    Slow but sure, that is the way to be.

## Comprehension Check

1. Which animals does Turtle see on his
    way to get a drink?
2. Why does Rabbit think he will get
    to the water before Turtle?
3. Did Turtle or Rabbit take more time
    to get to the water?
    Why did one of them take so long?

# Jump or Jiggle

by Evelyn Beyer

Frogs jump
Caterpillars hump

Worms wiggle
Bugs jiggle

Rabbits hop
Horses clop

Snakes slide
Seagulls glide

Mice creep
Deer leap

Puppies bounce
Kittens pounce

Lions stalk—
But—
I walk!

# The Fence

by Judith Herbst

Mr. Pocket lived in a big white house.
Amy lived in the blue house next door.
Mr. Pocket never talked to Amy.
He never talked to any of his neighbors.
Mr. Pocket did not like people.

One day Mr. Pocket started to build
something between his house and the road.
Amy saw Mr. Pocket work most of the day.
He worked until it was late.

"What are you doing?" asked Amy.

Mr. Pocket would not say a word.

The days went by one after another.
Mr. Pocket worked fast, and he worked
well.

People would stop and ask Mr. Pocket
what he was doing.

Most people asked how soon he would be
done.

But Mr. Pocket would not talk.

After a while, most people did not stop at
Mr. Pocket's house.

"We shall see what he has made after it is
done," they said to one another.

But Amy still saw Mr. Pocket work each
day until it was late.
Soon Amy could tell what Mr. Pocket was
building.
It was a great big fence.

The fence was long and tall.
It would go all around Mr. Pocket's house
after it was done.
There was not another fence like it.
The fence was well made and beautiful.

Amy saw how well made and beautiful the
fence was.
She told Mr. Pocket what she thought of
his fence.
Mr. Pocket did not say a word to Amy.
But Amy thought she saw Mr. Pocket start
to smile.

One day Amy was on her way to school.
She was thinking about the fence.

"No one has come to see the fence for a
long time," thought Amy.
"I shall tell Joe about it."

So Amy found Joe after school and said,
"Come and see Mr. Pocket's fence.
It goes in and out between the trees."

"Who wants to see an old fence?" asked
Joe.

"But this one is so well made!" said Amy.
"There is not another one like it."

Joe and Amy went to see the fence.

"This is a well-made fence," said Joe.
"It is the most beautiful fence around."

Joe told many other people about the
fence.
They came to see it.
Most of them said it was beautiful.

Mr. Pocket worked without saying a word.
But now and then he began to smile.

204

One day Mr. Pocket started to build a
gate for his fence.
It was the last thing he had to do.
Amy and Joe came to see Mr. Pocket work.
Amy's mother and father came too.
Mr. Pocket worked until it was late.
Then the gate was done.

Mr. Pocket looked up and said, "What are
you all doing here?"

"We came to see your beautiful fence,"
said Amy.

Mr. Pocket began to smile again.

"Shall I tell you something?" he asked.
"A fence should not stand between people.
I did not know that until now.
First I made my fence to keep people out.
But now this fence has a gate."

Mr. Pocket's smile was very big now.
He opened the gate and asked his
neighbors to come in.

**Comprehension Check**
1. Why did Mr. Pocket build a fence
   between his house and the road?
2. What did Amy think of the fence?
3. Why did Mr. Pocket open the gate
   after the fence was done?

# Jean Doesn't Need Help

adapted from a story by Ann Runck

Jean was seven.
She liked to do things by herself.
But too many people always wanted to
help her.
Jean's mother would try to help her.
Jean's father would try to help her.
Jean's grandmother would try to help her.
All that help made Jean angry.

One day Jean wanted to draw a picture by herself.

"Let me help you," said her father. "Here's some red and purple to use."

Jean looked angry. "I want to try it by myself," she said.

208

Another day Jean said, "I think I'll try
to skate."

"Let me help you," said her mother.
"I shall hold your hand.
I shall show you what to do."

Then Jean wanted to play football.
She wanted to try it by herself.

Her grandmother said, "I shall hold the
football for you."

Jean looked angry again.

"I want to do something all by myself,"
said Jean.
"I'll try to make a kite and fly it."

So Jean went upstairs.
She got some paper and some string.
Then she found some sticks outside.

"May we try to help you?" asked her
father.

"No, thank you," said Jean.
And she went upstairs again.

"She doesn't want our help," said
Jean's mother.

"No, she doesn't," said her father.

"Maybe she doesn't need so much help,"
said her grandmother.
"Too much help makes her angry.
We should let her do some things by
herself."

Jean made her kite with the paper,
string, and sticks.
The kite was beautiful.
And Jean made it by herself.

"This kite couldn't be better," said Jean.
"I'll try to fly it now that it is done."

Jean didn't look angry anymore.

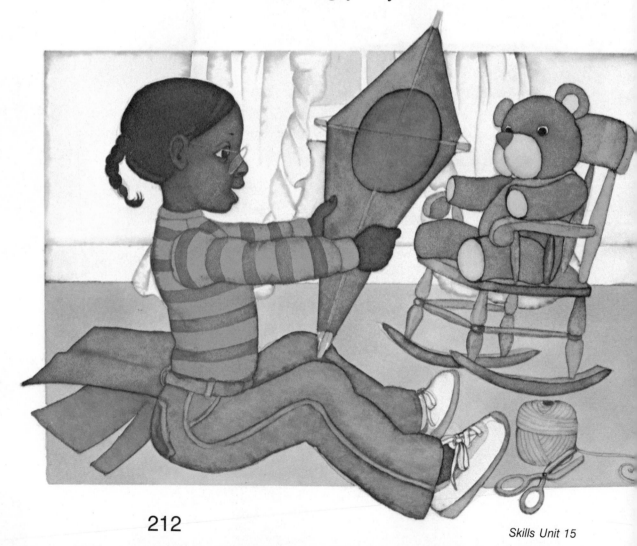

212

Jean got out her skates.
Then she went to the top of the house.
Jean went around and around the top of
the house on her skates.
The wind took her kite up in the air.
Jean went faster and faster.
She was flying her own kite by herself!

Jean's mother, father, and grandmother
went to the top of the house too.
They wanted to see Jean fly her kite.

"Jean doesn't need our help," said her mother.

"She doesn't look angry anymore," said her father.

"And just look at that kite!" said her grandmother.
"I couldn't make a kite like that by myself.
Maybe *I'll* ask Jean to help *me*!"

**Comprehension Check**

1. Why was Jean angry at first?
2. How did Jean's mother, father, and grandmother try to help her?
3. Why do you think Jean wanted to do things by herself?

214

# You Never Know What You Will Find

by Diana Heller

One day Ray and Sue wanted to do something after breakfast.

"Let's go down to the beach," said Sue.

"But I want to go to town," said Ray.

"You go to town almost every day," said their mother.
"Why not do something different today?"

"What's different about going to the beach?" asked Ray.

"You never know!" said their mother.
"Today just might be different."

So Ray and Sue started off to the beach.

"We'll see you in town in a little while," they called to their mother.

When they got to the beach, they saw something different.
There was a large bottle on the beach.
Ray and Sue picked up the bottle.
They saw a paper in it.

"Look at this!" said Ray.
"Maybe it's a clue to a treasure."

Sue and Ray took the paper out.
They saw some words on the paper.
It *was* a clue to a treasure.
This is what the paper said:

Go to the fence on Beach Road.
When you see the second large tree,
look above the cut on its tr

When Sue had read the clue, she said,
"There's a word missing.
The word must have something to do with a tree."

"Do you think it's *trail*?" asked Ray.

"No," said Sue, "I think it's *trunk*.
Trunk starts with tr.
Trunk has to do with a tree."

"Let's find that second tree!" said Ray.

Ray and Sue found the second tree when
they got to the fence.
They looked above the cut on its trunk.
There they saw a second paper.
It was a second clue to the treasure!
Sue and Ray read the second clue.
Here's what it said:

Go to the old red house.
Read what it says
above the front d

"The old red house is *our* house!" said
Ray.
"The word that starts with *d* is *door*."

Sue and Ray ran back to their house.
When they got there, they looked above
the front door.
They saw this:

Across from the house of Mr. Jones
Find a box among the st

"We're pretty good at this now,"
said Sue.
"I think the missing word is *stones*."

Ray and Sue looked for the box.
They found it among the large stones
across from Mr. Jones's house.
When they opened the box, they saw a
great treasure.

"I know who made those clues," said
Ray.

"And I know who put this treasure here,"
laughed Sue.
"Let's go find her in town!"

Ray and Sue ran to town.
When they got to town, they found their
mother.

"Thank you for the treasure," said Ray.

"We'll have fun with it for a long time,"
said Sue.

"You see," said their mother, "today
was different after all.
You never know what you will find!"

## Comprehension Check

1. Where did each of the clues tell Ray and
   Sue to go?
2. Why were they happy with their
   treasure?

# The Apple Tree Behind the House

by Joanne Barkan

There was an apple tree behind Paco's house.
It was Paco's own apple tree.
His mother and father planted the tree for Paco when he was very small.

Paco saw the tree grow little by little.
It became taller and taller, just as Paco became taller and taller.
Then, at last, apples began to grow on the tree.

"Just look at those apples on your tree,"
said Paco's father.
"They are small now.
But they will grow big and red.
Then you will be able to pick them."

The little apples did grow.
Soon they were large and red.

"Just look at those beautiful apples,"
said Paco's mother one day.
"When are you going to pick them?"

"I don't know," said Paco.
"Maybe it's still too soon."

The next day Mark came over.
"Just look at those big red apples,"
said Mark.
"Why don't we eat a few?"

"They do look good," said Paco.
"But maybe they will get even better.
Maybe it's too soon to pick them."

A few more days went by.

"What are you going to do about the
apples?" asked Paco's father.
"Don't you think it's time to pick them?"

"The apples will not be good in a while,"
said Paco's mother.
"They will fall off the tree.
Then it will be too late to eat them."

Paco looked at the apples and said again,
"But maybe it's still too soon."

That night Paco had a dream while he
was sleeping.
Paco had a dream about his apple tree.
This was Paco's dream:

Paco was standing under his tree.
First the top of the tree began to move.
Then the apple tree began to talk!

"I sure did grow apples," said the tree.
"Some people think apples are great.
But I say enough is enough!
Who wants to carry all these apples day
after day?
Doesn't that boy Paco know what to do
with an apple tree?"

Paco thought he should say something to
his tree.
"Say there, tree," began Paco.

228

"So it's *you*," said the tree.
"It's about time we had a talk.
Do you know how long I've had to carry
these apples?
Too long!
I'll have to let the apples fall if you
don't pick them now."

Paco looked at all the apples.

"I don't know which to pick," he said.
"Those on the right look good.
But maybe those on the left are better.
I don't know which to take."

"Right. Left. Front. Back," said the
tree.
"I just can't carry these apples anymore.
I need a rest!"

The tree began to let the apples fall.
They came down one after another.
Soon there were apples all around Paco's
feet.
There were no more apples on the tree.

And that was the end of Paco's dream.

230

The next day Paco ran outside as fast as
he could.
He ran behind the house.
There was his apple tree.
It was still full of large red apples.

Paco started to pick the apples.
His mother and father came out to help.

"It looks like you want these apples
now," said Paco's mother and father.

"I do want some apples," said Paco.
"And this apple tree wants a rest!"

**Comprehension Check**

1. Why did Paco's mother and father want
   Paco to pick the apples?
2. What did the tree say to Paco?
3. Can apple trees talk to people?
   When did the apple tree talk to Paco?

# One of Each, Please

by Marion Edey

A basket of apples stood in the shed.
"What beautiful apples!" Elizabeth said.
"Some of them yellow and some of them red."

"Which would you rather?"
said her father.

"The red ones are juicy," Elizabeth cried.
"But maybe the yellow are sweeter inside."
She looked and she looked
and she *couldn't* decide.

"Both of them, Father.
*That's* what I'd rather."

232

# Grand Teton National Park

by Christine Economos

The sun comes up.
It shines between the mountains and above
the blue lakes.
It shines between the trees in the woods.
The animals start to look for things to
eat.
The people get up in the little houses
along the lakes.
A new day is about to start at Grand
Teton National Park.

Grand Teton National Park is in Wyoming.
The park is different now from the way
it was awhile ago.
There were no houses for people to
stay in awhile ago.
There were not many trails through the
mountains awhile ago.
There were not many trails through the
woods awhile ago.

Now there are houses along the lakes.
There are trails all over the park.
Now people can come and stay at Grand
Teton for many days.

234

Many trails go through the mountains and
along the lakes.
Great trees stand along the trails.
Most people walk along the trails.
Others ride horses.
They all like to look at the beautiful
woods and the animals.
They also like the clean mountain air.

There are many mountains in the park.
The one called Grand Teton is the tallest.
There is snow on its top.

There are four lakes in the park too.
The water in the lakes is very clean.
Many people like to go in the water when
the weather is warm.

Deer, porcupines, rabbits, and turtles
are just some of the animals that live
in the park.
These animals roam through the woods.
They go down to the lakes to drink.
Many ducks fly through Grand Teton Park
on their way to warmer weather.
Some of them stop at the lakes to rest.

The animals find enough to eat in the
park most of the time.
But they did not have enough to eat one
time awhile ago.
It was very cold at Grand Teton that
time.
There was snow all over the park.
Many trees were torn up by the wind.
The animals could not find things to eat.
Many of them had to eat tree bark until
the weather became warmer.

There are people who live and work in the park all the time.

These people look after the park and its animals.

These people know when animals are born in the park.

They help animals that are hurt.

They show people through the park.

They look out for fires in the mountains.

The sun goes down behind the mountains
in the park.
This is very beautiful to see.
Some people build fires by the lake
after dark.
They use wood that is old.
They make things to eat on the fires.
Then they talk and sing.
This is a good way to end a day at
Grand Teton.

**Comprehension Check**
1. What do people do at Grand Teton?
2. What animals can you see along the
   trails?
3. How was Grand Teton different awhile
   ago?

# Animals You Can't See

by Timothy D. Loughman

All animals must eat something.
Many animals eat other animals.
They must do this to live.

But no animal *wants* to be another
animal's breakfast!
How does an animal stop other animals
from eating it?

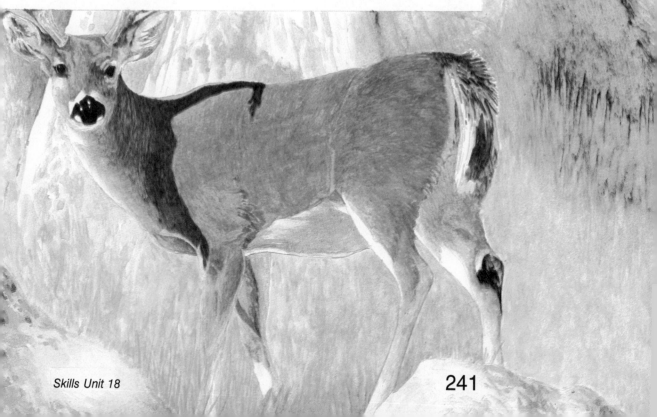

Animals can look just like the things
around them.
Then other animals can't see them very well.
The other animals will not be able to
find them.
It is important for many animals to look like
what is around them.

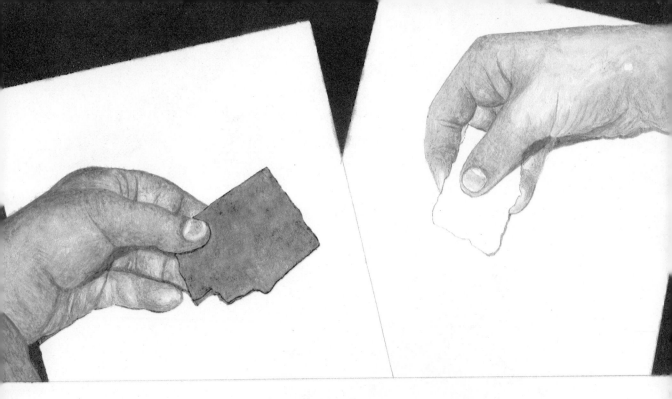

Here is something for you to try.
Put a small dark paper on a large
white paper.
Now put a small white paper on the
same large white paper.
Which small paper can you see better?
The dark one stands out.

Walk a few feet away from the papers.
Now you might not be able to see the
small white paper at all.
The small white paper looks just like
what is around it.

A bird can see a dark rabbit in the white
snow very well.
White rabbits do not stand out as much.
So some dark rabbits become white when
the snow starts to fall.
Those rabbits become dark again when
there is no more snow.
Other animals can't find the rabbits as
often this way.
This is very important to a rabbit!

244

Did you ever look at a butterfly's
wings?
Its wings may be orange or red on top.
But the undersides of its wings are often
dark like tree bark.
A butterfly often stands on tree bark.
It stands still with its wings together
over its back.
Other animals see only the undersides of
its wings.
Most birds flying above do not see the
butterfly at all.
So they look for other insects to eat.

Part of a little deer's fur is light
and part of it is dark.
The deer looks like the woods around it.
Other animals often don't see the deer.
This is important for a little deer.

246

It is important for many animals to look like the things around them.
But this is not always enough.
It is also important for some animals to stay very still.
They can find other animals to eat this way.

One insect looks just like a stick.
It stands very still.
It looks like the sticks around it.
Other insects often think it is a stick.
They walk right up to it.
Then, all at once, the stick moves.
The stick insect eats the other insects.

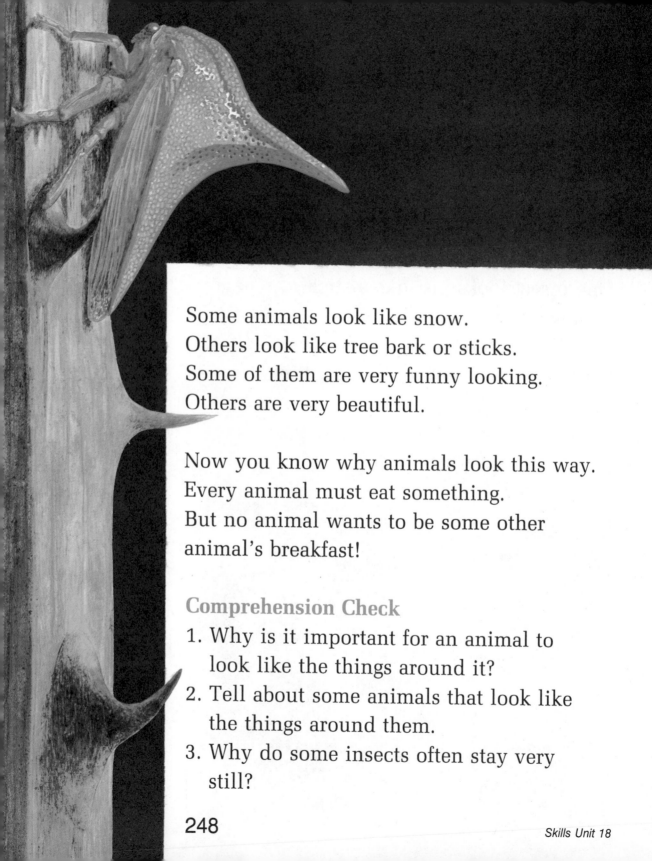

Some animals look like snow.
Others look like tree bark or sticks.
Some of them are very funny looking.
Others are very beautiful.

Now you know why animals look this way.
Every animal must eat something.
But no animal wants to be some other
animal's breakfast!

## Comprehension Check

1. Why is it important for an animal to
   look like the things around it?
2. Tell about some animals that look like
   the things around them.
3. Why do some insects often stay very
   still?

248

# Mr. Gumpy's Motor Car

by John Burningham

Mr. Gumpy was going for a ride in his
car.
He drove out of the gate and down the
lane.

"May we come too?" said the children.

"May we?" said the rabbit, the cat, the
dog, the pig, the sheep, the chickens,
the calf, and the goat.

"All right," said Mr. Gumpy.
"But it will be tight."

And they all piled in.

250

"It's a lovely day," said Mr. Gumpy.
"Let's take the old dirt road across
the fields."

For a while they drove along happily.
The sun shone, the engine chugged, and
everyone was enjoying the ride.

"I don't like the look of those clouds.
I think it's going to rain," said
Mr. Gumpy.

Very soon the dark clouds were right
overhead.
Mr. Gumpy stopped the car.
He jumped out, put up the top, and down
came the rain.
The road grew muddier and muddier, and
the wheels began to spin.

Mr. Gumpy looked at the hill ahead.

"Some of you will have to get out and push," he said.

"Not me," said the goat.
"I'm too old."

"Not me," said the calf.
"I'm too young."

"Not us," said the chickens.
"We can't push."

"Not me," said the sheep.
"I might catch cold."

"Not me," said the pig.
"I've a bone in my hoof."

"Not me," said the dog.
"But I'll drive if you like."

"Not me," said the cat.
"It would ruin my fur."

"Not me," said the rabbit.
"I'm not very well."

"Not me," said the girl.
"He's stronger."

"Not me," said the boy.
"She's bigger."

254

The wheels churned. . . .
The car sank deeper into the mud.

"Now we're really stuck," said
Mr. Gumpy.

They all got out and pushed.
They pushed and shoved and heaved
and strained and gasped and slipped
and slithered and squelched.

Slowly the car began to move. . . .

"Don't stop!" cried Mr. Gumpy.
"Keep it up!
We're nearly there."

Everyone gave a mighty heave—
the tires gripped. . . .
The car edged its way up to the top of
the hill.
They looked up and saw that the sun was
shining again.

It began to get hot.

"We'll drive home across the bridge,"
said Mr. Gumpy.
"Then you can go for a swim."

And they did.
After a while it was time to go home.

"Good-bye," said Mr. Gumpy.
"Come for a drive another day."

# Very Lovely

by Rose Fyleman

Wouldn't it be lovely if the rain came down
Til the water was quite high over all the town?
If the cars and buses all were set afloat,
And we had to go to school in a little boat?

Wouldn't it be lovely if it still should pour
And we all went up to live on the second floor?
If we saw the butcher sailing up the hill,
And we took the letters in at the window sill?

It's been raining, raining all the afternoon;
All these things might happen really very soon.
If we woke tomorrow and found they had begun,
Wouldn't it be glorious?
*Wouldn't* it be fun?

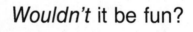

# Glossary

---
## A a
---

**above**  The butterfly is above the flower.

**apple**  An apple is a fruit that is good to eat. Apples grow on trees. **apples**

---
## B b
---

**bake**  Pam and her father bake some bread. They are baking it in the oven.

**beach**  A beach is a strip of land next to the water. Some beaches are sandy. **beaches**

**build**  Nadema is building a house. Next she will build a fence.

## C  c

**carry**  Ray is carrying a box. He will carry it into the house.

**children**  Children are young girls and young boys. Children grow up to be women and men.

# D d

dark

duck

**dark** It is dark outside after the sun goes down.

**deer** A deer is a wild animal. Many deer have antlers. **deer**

**door** You open a door to go into a building or a room. **doors**

**duck** A duck is a bird that swims and flies. Some ducks are wild. **ducks**

## E e

**eye** Your eye is in your face. You see with your eyes. **eyes**

## F f

**few** There are a few leaves on the tree.

**fire** A fire is made by burning something. Fires can be dangerous. **fires**

## G g

**gate** A gate is a door in a wall or fence. **gates**

**grow** The sunflower is growing fast. It will grow very tall.

---
# H  h
---

**horse** A horse can carry a person or pull a wagon. Some horses do tricks. **horses**

---
# I  i
---

**insect** An insect is any small animal with six legs. Flies and bees are insects. **insects**

---
# J  j
---

**just** Pam has just come home from the beach.

kite

leaf

**kite**  A kite will fly on a windy day. Sometimes kites get caught in trees. **kites**

**late**  Mark is late for the show.

**leaf**  A leaf is part of a tree or plant. A tree has many leaves. **leaves**

# M  m

**move**  A new family is about to move into this building. Another family is moving out.

# N  n

**neighbor**  A neighbor is someone who lives nearby. These neighbors are working in their yards. **neighbors**

# O  o

**outside**  Jim's friends are outside.

**P  p**

**paper**  You can write on paper. You can wrap something in paper too. **papers**

**plant**  Mother is planting trees. She will plant them in the front yard and in the backyard.

**Q  q**

**quill**  A quill is very sharp. A porcupine is covered with quills. Sometimes the quills stick out. **quills**

# R  r

rain  Water from the clouds is rain.
This girl is walking in the rain.

# S  s

school  Children go to school to learn.
schools

sleep  The baby is sleeping. He sleeps
for a long time each day.

stick  A stick is a long, thin piece of
wood. sticks

sun

use

sun  The sun makes the light every day.

---

# T  t

---

tall  Father is tall. He is taller than Kim.

tell  Jan is telling a story to her friends. Jan likes to tell stories.

---

# U  u

---

use  The girl is using paint to make a picture. She will use blue and red.

# V v

very

yes

**very** It is very cold and very windy outside.

# W w

**water** You can drink water. You can wash your hands in water.

**wing** A wing is a part of a bird. A bird uses its wings to fly. **wings**

# Y y

**yes** Yes can be an answer to a question. Yes means you agree. Lanu said, "Yes, I do like apples."

# MASTERY WORD LIST

The following high-frequency words (words that appear on recognized word-frequency lists) have been read a minimum of six times by the end of this book. Pupils should be able to recognize both the root word and the root word with these endings: *s, es, ed, ing, 's, est.*

The page number printed after each word shows the word's first appearance in this book. For a cumulative list of mastery words see the Teacher's Edition for *Kick Up Your Heels.*

| | | | |
|---|---|---|---|
| quills 24 | duckling 59 | because 92 | foal 155 |
| other 24 | just 59 | late 92 | each 155 |
| full 24 | duck 60 | school 92 | able 156 |
| of 24 | use 61 | show 92 | among 157 |
| hurt 24 | ugly 66 | leather 100 | rest 164 |
| sharp 24 | weather 76 | tell 110 | door 173 |
| tree 25 | air 76 | before 110 | few 173 |
| long 25 | or 76 | cannot 110 | back 173 |
| fight 26 | rain 76 | yes 111 | still 173 |
| right 27 | fall 76 | bake 111 | does 173 |
| pick 28 | outside 76 | bread 111 | without 174 |
| special 32 | room 77 | enough 111 | anything 174 |
| read 32 | balloon 77 | clean 116 | stage 181 |
| very 32 | number 78 | sure 118 | only 181 |
| from 32 | goes 78 | its 118 | then 182 |
| closed 33 | almost 80 | carry 118 | part 183 |
| front 33 | once 84 | myself 118 | word 185 |
| again 34 | elves 85 | them 118 | between 199 |
| left 45 | night 85 | our 119 | most 199 |
| always 50 | might 85 | neighbor 119 | until 199 |
| around 50 | while 85 | become 123 | another 200 |
| why 50 | became 85 | ranch 147 | well 200 |
| should 50 | large 85 | think 147 | done 200 |
| end 50 | such 86 | let 148 | shall 201 |
| thought 51 | already 92 | across 148 | doesn't 207 |
| warm 58 | sleep 92 | road 149 | herself 207 |
| also 58 | even 92 | own 155 | try 207 |

(acknowledgments continued from page 2)

ILLUSTRATIONS

Cover: Bobbye Cochrane
Pages 8-14, Jennie Williams; page 15, Angela Adams; pages 16-22,
Helen Tullen; page 23, Joan Goodman; pages 24–31, Pam Carroll;
pages 32–39, Angela Adams; pages 40–49, Jared Lee; pages 50–57,
Lane Yerkes; pages 58–65, Marie DeJohn; pages 66–74, Ed Parker;
page 75, Stella Ormai; pages 76–83, Ronald Himler; pages 84–91,
Jared Lee; pages 92–99, Les Morrill; pages 100–109, Monica Santa;
pages 118–125, Lane Yerkes; pages 126–134, Arnold Lobel;
pages 136–145, Rosekrans Hoffman; page 146, Ronald Himler;
pages 155–162, Raphael and Bolognese; pages 163–172, Miriam Schottland;
pages 173–180, Margot Apple; pages 181–188, Marie DeJohn; pages 189–
197, Joe Veno; page 198, Ron LeHew; pages 199–206, Ed Parker; pages
207–214, Angela Adams; pages 215–222, James Watling; pages 223–231,
Joan Goodman; page 232, Debbie Sims; pages 241–248, Jon R. Freidman;
pages 249–257, John Burningham; page 258, Bob Barner; pages 259–272,
Joe Veno.

PHOTOGRAPHS

Pages 110–117, Stephan Tur; page 147 (top), Jim Amos, *Photo
Researchers, Inc.*; page 147 (bottom), *The Bettmann Archive*; page
148, J. Wright, *Bruce Coleman, Inc.*; page 149, Nicholas de Vore III,
*Bruce Coleman, Inc.*; page 150, Jonathan Wright, *Bruce Coleman, Inc.*;
page 151, J. Rychetnik, *Photo Researchers, Inc.*; page 152, Jonathan
Wright, *Bruce Coleman, Inc.*; page 153, Robert Davis, *Photo
Researchers, Inc.*; page 154, Rod Hanna, *Woodfin Camp & Assoc.*; page
233, Porterfield-Checkering, *Photo Researchers, Inc.*; page 234,
L. Lee Rue III, *Bruce Coleman, Inc.*; page 235, Nicholas de Vore III,
*Bruce Coleman, Inc.*; page 236, Helen Williams, *Photo Researchers,
Inc.*; page 236, Kenneth W. Fink, *Bruce Coleman, Inc.*; page 237,
Steven C. Kaufman, *Photo Researchers, Inc.*; page 237, Tom McHugh,
*Photo Researchers, Inc.*; page 238, John V. A. F. Neal, *Photo
Researchers, Inc.*; page 239, William J. Jahoda, *Photo Researchers,
Inc.*; page 240, Jeff Foott, *Bruce Coleman, Inc.*

STUDIO

Kirchoff/Wohlberg, Inc.